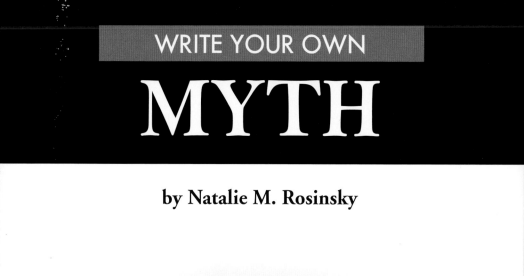

# WRITE YOUR OWN
# MYTH

by Natalie M. Rosinsky

Compass Point Books ✦ Minneapolis, Minnesota

Compass Point Books
3109 West 50th Street, #115
Minneapolis, MN 55410

 This book was manufactured with paper containing
at least 10 percent post-consumer waste.

Managing Editor: Catherine Neitge
Designer: ticktock Entertainment Ltd
Page Production: Bobbie Nuytten
Photo Researcher: Svetlana Zhurkin
Library Consultant: Kathleen Baxter

Art Director: Jaime Martens
Creative Director: Keith Griffin
Editorial Director: Nick Healy

Compass Point Books would like to acknowledge the contributions of Tish Farrell, who
authored earlier Write Your Own books and whose supporting text is reused in part herein.

**Library of Congress Cataloging-in-Publication Data**
Rosinsky, Natalie M. (Natalie Myra)
  Write your own myth / by Natalie M. Rosinsky.
    p. cm. — (Write your own)
  Includes bibliographical references and index.
  ISBN-13: 978-0-7565-3372-4 (library binding)
  ISBN-10: 0-7565-3372-4 (library binding)
  1. Authorship—Juvenile literature. 2. Myth—Juvenile literature. I. Title. II. Series.
PN171.M93R67 2007
808'.02—dc22                    2007011472

Visit Compass Point Books on the Internet at *www.compasspointbooks.com*
or e-mail your request to *custserv@compasspointbooks.com*

About the Author
Natalie M. Rosinsky is the award-winning author of
more than 100 works for young readers. She earned
graduate degrees from the University of Wisconsin-
Madison and has been a high school teacher and
college professor as well as a corporate trainer. Natalie,
who reads and writes in Mankato, Minnesota, says,
"My love of reading led me to write. I take pleasure in
framing ideas, crafting words, detailing other lives and
places. I am delighted to share these joys with young
authors in the Write Your Own series of books."

## Be Wonderfully Creative

*How did the world begin? Why are there stars in the sky? What makes one person have good luck and someone else have bad luck? What happens after death?*

*For thousands of years, people around the globe have wondered about these questions and other great mysteries. Seeking answers, they told stories about gods and goddesses, heroes and monsters, spirits and fantastic creatures. These tales are the heart of the world's many mythologies and religions. For some people, these ancient myths still hold religious truth.*

*While science today provides answers to some of those great mysteries, people still enjoy telling and retelling myths. You, too, can write your own myth! This book contains brainstorming and training activities to sharpen your writing skills. Tips and advice from famous writers and examples from their own work will help you join the grand tradition of mythmaking and be wonderfully creative.*

# CONTENTS

# HOW TO USE THIS BOOK

## WANT TO BE A WRITER?

This book is the perfect place to start. It aims to give you the tools to write your own myth. Learn how to craft believable portraits of people and perfect plots with satisfying beginnings, middles, and endings. Examples from famous books appear throughout, with tips and techniques from published authors to help you on your way.

## Get the writing habit

Do timed and regular practice. Real writers learn to write even when they don't particularly feel like it.

Create a myth-writing zone.

Keep a journal.

Carry a notebook—record interesting events and note how people behave and speak.

## Generate ideas

Find a myth you want to tell or retell. What are the questions it answers?

Think of a person or character whose story you want to tell. What are his or her problems and accomplishments?

Brainstorm to find out everything about your chosen myth or person.

Research settings, events, and people related to the myth or person.

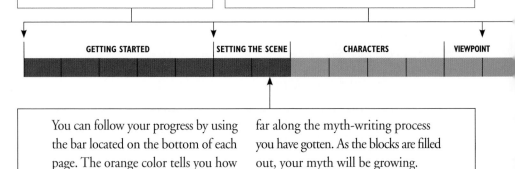

GETTING STARTED          SETTING THE SCENE          CHARACTERS          VIEWPOINT

You can follow your progress by using the bar located on the bottom of each page. The orange color tells you how far along the myth-writing process you have gotten. As the blocks are filled out, your myth will be growing.

4

## Plan

What is your myth about?

What happens?

Plan beginning, middle, and end.

Write a synopsis or create storyboards.

## Write

Write the first draft, then put it aside for a while.

Check spelling and dialogue —does it flow?

Remove unnecessary words.

Does the myth have a good title and satisfying ending?

Avoid clichés.

## Publish

Write or print the final draft.

Always keep a copy for yourself.

Send your myth to children's magazines, Internet writing sites, competitions, or school magazines.

SYNOPSES AND PLOTS | WINNING WORDS | SCINTILLATING SPEECH | HINTS AND TIPS | THE NEXT STEP

When you get to the end of the bar, your book is ready to go! You are an author! You now need to decide what to do with your book and what your next project should be. Perhaps it will be a sequel to this myth, or maybe something completely different.

## YOUR CREATIVE LIFESTYLE

**M**odern myth writers may do research in the library or on the Internet. They may travel to interview storytellers from a different tradition or to see the locations mentioned in particular myths. Just like all writers, mythmakers need handy tools and a safe, comfortable place for their work. A computer can make writing quicker, but it is not essential.

### What you need

These materials will help you organize your ideas and your findings:

- small notebook that you carry everywhere
- paper for writing activities
- pencils, pens, or markers with different colored ink
- index cards for recording facts and myths
- files or folders to keep your gathered information organized and safe
- dictionary, thesaurus, and encyclopedia

### Find your writing place

Think about where you as a writer feel most comfortable and creative. Perhaps a spot in your bedroom works best for you. Possibly a corner in the public library is better.

If your writing place is outside your home, store your writing materials in a take-along bag or backpack.

## Create a myth-writing zone

- Play some of your favorite music or music from the tradition whose myths you are learning and retelling.
- Use earplugs if you write best when it is quiet.
- Decorate your space with pictures of places mentioned in myths or of art based on mythical characters and events.
- Place objects that hold good memories from your own life around your space.

## Follow the writer's golden rule

Once you have chosen your writing space, go there regularly and often. It is all right to do other kinds of writing there—such as a diary or letters—*as long as you keep on writing!*

**CASE STUDY**

Mary Pope Osborne, author of myths as well as the popular Magic Tree House series of books, is unusual in her writing habits. She creates her own writing zone wherever she goes. She admits, "No two days of writing for the last 20 odd years have been the same. I write at every time of the day. I carry my laptop to every part of the house—or to places outside the house. I'm a creature of constant change."

# GET THE WRITING HABIT

**B**efore you can write fascinating myths, you have to build up your writing "muscles." Just as an athlete lifts weights or a musician practices scales, you must train regularly. You cannot wait until you are in the mood or feel inspired.

### Tips and techniques

Set a regular amount of time and a schedule for your writing. It could be 10 minutes every morning before breakfast or one hour twice a week after supper. Then, come rain or shine, stick to your schedule.

## Now it's your turn

### See stories in the stars

Be inspired the way many ancient people were. Find a safe place to gaze at the dark night sky. Or grab a star atlas from the library or Internet to view scenes of the heavens above you. People throughout the world have used their imaginations to see pictures in the groups of stars—called constellations—that cluster together. They then created myths about these constellations. What pictures do you see when you look at the stars? Gaze all around or focus in on one of the constellations already named.

Now that you are starry-eyed, begin your writing practice with some timed brainstorming. Spend 10 minutes in your writing place. Jot down everything that comes into your head when you think of patterns in the night sky. Some of the names already given to constellations such as the Great Bear might inspire you. What adventures can you imagine involving a large bear? Scribble quickly! Do not worry about correct grammar or punctuation. Let your ideas flow like bright, bubbling juice poured from a large pitcher. You are on your way to being a writer of myths!

### CASE STUDY

Author Mary Pope Osborne became fascinated by mythology in college. She says its "realm of adventure and changing scenery" led her to become a religion major and learn "as much as I could about other cultures." Nowadays, she says, "Without even leaving my home I've traveled around the globe, learning about the religions of the world."

# GIVING LIFE TO MYTHS

**P**eople around the world often believed that gods and goddesses had their own special powers and interests in the world. For instance, the earth and sky usually "belonged" to different deities. The Greeks and Romans had different names for their gods, but the stories they told about them were similar.

Mythmakers assigned human emotions, motives, and family relationships to the gods they worshipped. Jealousy of his half-brothers led the Norse god Loki to commit evil deeds. Bad temper caused the Hindu god Shiva of India to attack and almost kill his wife's son, Ganesh. A mother's love for her daughter caused the Greek goddess Demeter to rescue Persephone—thereby, according to myth, restoring fruitful spring and summer to the world. In many myths, romantic love between gods or goddesses and humans has dramatic and surprising consequences. Some of the family dramas and romances of myth could be part of today's TV soap operas or tell-all talk shows!

## Now it's your turn

### See the stories around you

Observe your friends, family, and neighbors. What dramas and romances do you see around you? Are there any comedies? Who is acting bravely, wisely, or generously? Who is behaving in a cowardly, foolish, or selfish way? Is anyone being silly? Whose successes or failures have touched your own life? Who is facing an important or difficult decision? Perhaps it is you! These stories all around you can help you brainstorm the central characters and events in your myth. Spend 15 minutes in your writing place. Jot down as many answers as you can to one or more of these questions. You are now ready to select the human elements that will give life to your myth.

## Now it's your turn

### Adventure into the realm of myth

Be as adventurous as any mythological hero. Dare to explore a new world of myth. Read myths from a continent or culture that is unknown to you. Or find and read myths with the same theme—such as storms, earthquakes, or the changing seasons—from five different cultures or countries. Are these myths told in different voices? In what other ways are they alike or different? By increasing the myths you know, you will win a hero's reward—new ideas and models for writing your own tale.

### CASE STUDY

Being responsible for a younger brother or sister is an important part of two modern novels rooted in myths. In *The Sea of Trolls*, Nancy Farmer combines Norse mythology with the adventures of 11-year-old Jack and his 5-year-old sister. In *Hippolyta and the Curse of the Amazons*, authors Jane Yolen and Robert J. Harris combine Greek mythology with 13-year-old Hippolyta's problems with her baby brother.

| SYNOPSES AND PLOTS | WINNING WORDS | SCINTILLATING SPEECH | HINTS AND TIPS | THE NEXT STEP |
|---|---|---|---|---|

# FIND YOUR VOICE

**R**eading many books will help you discover your own style of writing—your writer's voice. Every good writer has a style of writing that is unique to that person. It takes lots of practice to acquire this voice. Writers continue to develop their voices throughout their lives. Skilled writers also learn to change their voices to match different subjects.

## Finding your writer's voice

Once you start reading as a writer, you will notice how writers have their own rhythm, style, and range of language that stay the same throughout a book. Kate McMullan, the author of *Have a Hot Time, Hades!*, has a playful, casual voice that is nothing like the serious, formal one Virginia Hamilton uses for an Egyptian myth in her collection, *In the Beginning: Creation Stories from Around the World*. Yet Hamilton uses a sly voice when she retells a humorous African myth in that book. Learning to recognize the different techniques writers use to craft their books is like learning to identify different kinds of music.

## Experiment

You may usually read only myths or adventure stories. Try other genres to see how authors of biography or science fiction, for example, write with their unique voices. You may find inspiration in how James Cross Giblin, the author of *Good Brother, Bad Brother: The Story of Edwin Booth and John Wilkes Booth*, crafted this biography of Abraham Lincoln's assassin and his family. You might discover writing tips while reading about the outer space journeys of the Dingillian family, characters created by science fiction writer David Gerrold.

## Writers' voices

Look at the kinds of words these authors use. Do they use lots of adjectives? What about the length and rhythm of their sentences? Which style do you prefer to read?

**Virginia Hamilton retells an Egyptian myth about the beginning of the world:**

*God Ra spoke these words:*
*"Many were the beings that came out of my mouth. This was before there was a heaven, before earth came into being, and before the ground and creeping things were created. Then they, too, started into being."*

Virginia Hamilton, "The Sun-God and the Dragon," in *In the Beginning: Creation Stories from Around the World*

**Kate McMullan retells Greek myths about the origin of the world, including this evil figure:**

*Call me Hades. My full name—His Royal Lowness, Lord of the Dead, King Hades—is a bit of a mouthful.*
Kate McMullan, *Have a Hot Time, Hades!*

**Joseph Bruchac retells a Cherokee myth about the stars and the early people:**

*This is what the old people told me when I was a child. Long ago when the world was new, there were not many stars in the sky. In those days the people depended on corn for their food. They would grind it and keep it in bins behind their homes. Bread made from the cornmeal often kept them from starving during the long winter months.*
Joseph Bruchac and Gayle Ross, *The Story of the Milky Way: A Cherokee Tale*

**Virginia Hamilton retells a creation myth from the Togo people of West Africa:**

*In the beginning, God was Wul-bar-i. And God Wulbari was heaven—spread not five feet above the mother, earth. The God was very upset. There was not enough space between Him and earth. The man who lived on earth kept bumping his head against the God. It didn't seem to bother the man, but it surely bothered Wulbari.*
Virginia Hamilton, "Spider Anansi Finds Something," in *In the Beginning: Creation Stories from Around the World*

# GET YOUR FACTS STRAIGHT

**A**void errors or *myth-stakes*. (Sorry!) Use library materials or the Internet to gather all the information you need to write your own myth. This includes information about how the people who first told this myth lived—what they wore and ate, what their homes were like, what games kids played and jobs adults had. Knowing about any important historical events that happened then—such as wars or earthquakes—is also useful.

## Get expert advice

If you heard your myth from a storyteller born into its traditions, ask this person to provide and check facts. Remember to thank your expert again!

## Mismatched and missing myths

Turn a potential problem into a pleasure. Because myths were told long before they were ever written down, some traditions have different versions of the same myth. Choose the version that works best with the human story that also interests you. Or, be inspired by thinking about the different versions and their possible origins. In Norse mythology, trolls are usually ugly, but a few Norse myths describe trolls as exceptionally beautiful. Nancy Farmer makes the way an ugly troll queen cruelly acquires and uses her beauty an important part of *The Sea of Trolls*.

**CASE STUDY**

In *Odysseus in the Serpent Maze*, Jane Yolen and Robert J. Harris say they use what archeologists have discovered about life in ancient Greece to get their facts straight. In *The Sea of Trolls*, Nancy Farmer reports researching historical information about the first Viking attack on England for her novel.

### Tips and techniques
Carry a notebook and pen with you at all times. Jot down sights, sounds, and even conversations that catch your attention. You never know when real life will provide inspiration for your mythmaking.

## Now it's your turn

### Think outside the myth!

Brainstorm about your favorite myth or adult mythical character. Imagine what happened in the hours or days before a myth began or in the time following it. Spend 10 minutes in your myth-writing place to capture your ideas on paper. Your own myth could be the prequel or sequel you just brainstormed.

Write down five words that describe a mythical character's personality and deeds. Would this character have had the same traits as a child or teen? What might have happened to make this character into the person—or creature—that myths reveal?

Take 10 minutes to scribble ideas for a brand-new story about this mythical character's early life.

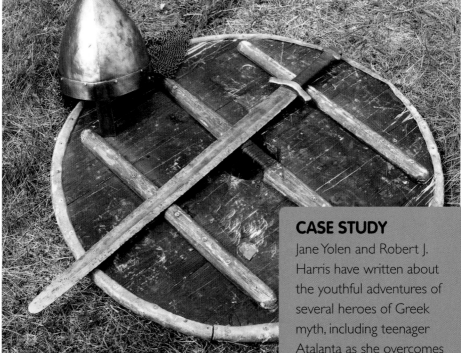

### CASE STUDY

Jane Yolen and Robert J. Harris have written about the youthful adventures of several heroes of Greek myth, including teenager Atalanta as she overcomes the Arcadian Beast.

## MANY WONDERFUL WORLDS

**A**s a myth writer, you set the scene in many wonderful worlds. The natural world that inspired the first myths is just one of the settings to create for readers. Your characters also journey outside this realm of ordinary experience. Their amazing adventures with gods and goddesses, monsters and other fantastic creatures call upon your imagination as well as your research and writing skills. Your efforts will help readers experience worlds imagined first by ancient people and now re-created by you with your own added flair.

### Sensational nature

In myths, the natural world is sensed in all its glory by the gods as well as humans. Donna Jo Napoli describes in vivid detail how the Greek god Pan responds to the changing seasons. This god of pastures and the flute, born half-man and half-goat, observes:

> *My reed flute relents, just as nature must. The east wind, Eurus, comes off the Aegean Sea, across the plains, carrying warm wetness to the waiting earth. I play the stirring of the roots within the soil, the rainbow colors of the early-spring flowers, the buzz of the bees, the whir of hummingbird wings, the willowy spring of newborn hedgehogs' spines.*
> Donna Jo Napoli, *The Great God Pan*

Readers can feel, see, and hear springtime come to the Greek island setting of this myth.

### *Now it's your turn*

**Be sensational!**

Learn all you can about the natural setting of your myths. A firsthand visit would be great, but research in the library or on the Internet is also worthwhile. Here are things to look for:

- photographs taken in different seasons showing the scenery as well as plants and fruits
- lists of wildlife that live there in different seasons
- recordings of wildlife sounds
- written descriptions of locations, wildlife, and changing seasons by scientists, fiction writers, and travelers

As you look at photographs and listen to recordings, jot down the words and impressions that your excited senses bring to mind. List as many sights and sounds as you can. Besides these, can you imagine and describe what the ripening fruit in a picture would taste like? What pleasant or unpleasant smells might accompany a herd of cattle? Beyond the sparkle displayed by winter ice, how might it feel on your hands or face? Include taste, smell, and touch in your sensational description of your myth's setting.

## CASE STUDY

For *The Great God Pan*, Donna Jo Napoli added firsthand knowledge of goats to her research. She lived on a farm the summer her youngest son was born. The care of goat hooves there was one of the jobs she "thought was most amazing."

### *Tips and techniques*

Check your facts. If you are writing about a herd of cattle or a school of dolphins, be sure you really know how these animals move and behave in groups. Use the library or Internet for information.

# AMAZING SIGHTS AND SOUNDS

**I**n myths, amazing events take place—often the result of very human emotions and relationships. In Greek myth, Phaeton is the son of the sun god Apollo and a human woman. When Phaeton foolishly thinks he is old and strong enough to drive the chariot of the sun, disaster strikes. Michael Cadmun describes the results in the far north as the chariot plunges downward:

> *It could have been a moment, or it could have been an hour, as the shock of the chariot's heat steamed the frozen waste. White-pelted bears dived into the seas, the water in turmoil under the sudden flood of ice melt. Avalanches tumbled down the face of virgin mountains, glaciers heaving into pieces, icebergs cascading. The tusked walruses floundered, simmering in brine.*
> Michael Cadmun, *Starfall: Phaeton and the Chariot of the Sun*

## CASE STUDY

Mary Pope Osborne says that the "best part of being a writer is being transported to other places and living other experiences." She surrounds herself "with the smells, weather, and people of imaginary landscapes."

## A history of inspiration

Myths inspire artists as well as writers. Painters, sculptors, vase makers, and weavers around the globe have all portrayed mythical figures and events. Sometimes, these images are even used in clothing and jewelry. The immortal phoenix, a bird reborn in fire, is associated with two different sun gods— Egyptian Ra and the Greek god Apollo. Composers of music also draw upon myth for some of their work.

## CASE STUDY

Michael Cadmun says, "Myths are a way of writing the truth without being tedious." Instead of explaining that foolish daring often leads to "misfortune" and that "parents can be as foolish as their children," Cadmun uses myth. He retells the tale of Apollo's giving in to Phaeton's plea to drive the sun chariot.

## Now it's your turn

### Look or listen again

Go to a museum to get new inspiration for your myth's setting. See how sculptors, painters, or craft makers imagined the people, places, and events in myth. Do their depictions match what you had in mind? Jot down 10 words or phrases that enter your head as you view an artwork related to myth. Use this list as you write or rewrite the setting.

In the library or on the Internet, find any music that your myth or its tradition has inspired. Listen to this music for further ideas. Jot down words or phrases that come to mind as you hear these musical myths.

## DISCOVER YOUR HERO

**Y**our hero is the lead figure in your myth. Whether you choose a human, a god or goddess, or even a fantastic creature as the hero, your job is to make readers know and care about this character. To have this connection, they need to understand what the hero thinks and feels.

### What is the problem?

A hero faces problems. In Greek myth, Orpheus is a musician whose young wife Eurydice dies. Sick at heart, Orpheus bravely journeys to the Underworld hoping to bring Eurydice back to life. In a Muskogee (Creek) tale, the Girl Who Helped Thunder is a fine hunter who is ignored just because she is female. The girl does not give up, however, and her quick wit and sharp eye win an important ally, Thunder. Together, they battle and defeat enemies of the Creek.

> *From high above, the Girl Who Helped Thunder lifted her bow and began firing white-hot bolts of lightning. Thunder rolled as her arrows exploded at the foot of the enemy.*
> Joseph Bruchac and Gayle Ross, *The Girl Who Married the Moon: Tales from Native North America*

Christopher Tebbett's modern hero, 14-year-old Zack Gilman, has recently lost his mother to cancer. Zack also has difficulties at school and at home because he dislikes sports. He deals with bullies and with disappointing his father, who loves football. When Zack meets the Norse gods in The Viking series, these problems become matters of life and death.

In Rick Riordan's modern-day novels, 12-year-old Perseus "Percy" Jackson copes with having attention deficit disorder and dyslexia. Then he finds himself at the center of a battle among the ancient Greek gods!

**CASE STUDY**

Rick Riordan's novel *The Lightning Thief* began as bedtime stories he told to his 8-year-old son. After the boy was diagnosed with attention deficit disorder and dyslexia, Riordan combined the Greek myths his son enjoyed with tales about Percy Jackson, a character with personal challenges like his son's.

## Now it's your turn

**Being strong and brave**

Heroes may perform daring deeds of physical strength and bravery. Sometimes, though, the monsters they battle are less obvious. Overcoming the prejudices and low opinions of others takes a different kind of courage and determination. Dealing with grief or learning disorders requires inner strength. Which kind of battles will your hero fight? Brainstorm and make a list of the problems your hero faces. Try to give this character more than one kind of battle to fight.

# REVEAL YOUR HERO'S WEAKNESSES

**H**eroes—just like all of us—have weaknesses. When you reveal your hero's flaws, readers can believe in and identify with this character. Brave Orpheus is so eager to see Eurydice that he disobeys instructions given by Hades, god of the Underworld. This failure causes Orpheus to lose Eurydice again.

In another Greek myth, young Odysseus sometimes takes needless risks and brags about his achievements. He hurts his friend Mentor by not including Mentor's brave deeds in his account of their adventures:

> *But when Odysseus looked over to where Mentor was sitting, his friend had turned his face away. Odysseus felt a stab of pain in his thigh, as though he'd been wounded a second time.*
> Jane Yolen and Robert J. Harris, *Odysseus in the Serpent Maze*

Recognizing his mistake, Odysseus stops boasting. He adds Mentor's accomplishments to the tale, and the two boys remain close friends. Authors Yolen and Harris show readers not only their hero's flaw but his effort to change this weakness.

### Tips and techniques
Give your hero at least one weakness—a so-called Achilles' heel. Greek myths say that the hero Achilles died when an arrow pierced his heel. This was the only part of his body that Achilles' mother forgot to wet as she held infant Achilles by his foot and dipped him into magical water that protected him from harm.

### Tips and techniques

*Help readers know what your hero looks like. Have other characters describe this character in dialogue. Or your hero could think about his or her appearance while looking in a mirror or pool of water.*

## Create your villain

Your villain provides a conflict or external problem that the hero must face. In myths, some difficulties considered beyond the control of individuals —such as war or natural disasters—are said to be caused by the gods. This is important to remember as you create a villain who opposes and challenges your hero.

## What is the motive?

In myths, people and the gods commit evil deeds for different reasons. Are they motivated by greed or jealousy? By the desire for power or fame? Or do they believe that their acts are not really evil at all? If a fantastic creature feeds upon people as well as cattle, is that hungry monster truly evil? Create a believable villain by showing this character's motives.

## Human evil

Greedy pirates think that no one will ransom young Odysseus:
*Three men grabbed Odysseus and dragged him to the ship's side.
He tried to wrench free, but he hadn't the strength, having spent
a night in the water. Besides, they were grown men.* Large *grown*
*men.* Large grown men with muscles. *In a moment, they had him
over their heads and were about to toss him overboard.*
Jane Yolen and Robert J. Harris, *Odysseus in the Serpent Maze*

## A god with human emotions

Sly Norse god Loki is jealous of his half-brother Balder's fame:
*Loki placed the piece of mistletoe in Hod's hand. Then he directed
Hod's aim and helped him send the mistletoe toward Balder.
The sharp sprig sailed through the air and lodged in Balder's heart.
At once, Balder fell to the ground, dead.*
Mary Pope Osborne, "The Death of Balder," in *Favorite
Norse Myths*

GETTING STARTED | SETTING THE SCENE | CHARACTERS | VIEWPOINT

### Natural disasters caused by gods or goddesses

*That night, the wind began to shriek. Athena, furious at the violence committed in her temple during Troy's sack, let loose her rage in a tremendous storm. Scores of ships sank or were splintered on the rocks. Floating bodies choked inlets and washed up in hundreds on the beaches.*
Paul Fleischman, *Dateline: Troy*

### Monstrous attacker

The god Hades sends his watchdog, a hellhound, to attack and feed on Percy:
*There on the rocks just above us was a black hound the size of a rhino, with lava-red eyes and fangs like daggers.*
*It was looking straight at me.*
Rick Riordan, *The Lightning Thief*

## Now it's your turn

### Hold a mirror up to evil!

In Greek myth, glancing into the terrible Medusa's eyes turned people to stone. The hero Perseus slew Medusa by looking into a mirror to aim his sword at her head. Now it is your turn to create such spectacular villains and heroes.

On two sheets of paper, draw five lines down and five lines across. In the top six boxes, write the words Physical Appearance, Clothing, Favorite Things, Motives, Flaws or Weaknesses, and Strengths or Powers. Now use one sheet to fill in ideas you have about your villain. Use the second sheet to brainstorm ideas about your hero.

When you are done, you will have 30 pieces of information about these important characters. You may use some of these ideas and throw others away. Perhaps some will give you the glimmer of new ideas to pursue.

# DEVELOP A SUPPORTING CAST

**H**ow your hero interacts with other characters tells a great deal about this person. You can add details or descriptions that bring minor characters to life. Just a sentence or two, or even a few words, can make an enormous difference.

## Now it's your turn

**Do "write" by minor characters**
Create at least one memorable trait for each minor character in your myth.

The personality of Odysseus' caregiver is communicated by the folk sayings the old woman always adds on to her remarks:

> *"Hold still, Master Odysseus,"*
> *his mother's old nurse, Menaera,*
> *snapped impatiently as she bathed*
> *his leg with cold water. "The*
> *wind may make the tree's branches*
> *tremble, but it cannot heal the*
> *broken limb."*
> Jane Yolen and Robert J. Harris,
> *Odysseus in the Serpent Maze*

Percy Jackson's friend Grover has successfully pretended to be a 14-year-old boy instead of the mythological, goat-footed creature he really is. Details reveal his disguise and personality:

> "I'm sorry," Grover sniffled. "I'm a failure. I'm—I'm the worst satyr in the world." He moaned, stomping his foot so hard it came off. I mean, the Converse hi-top came off. The inside was filled with Styrofoam, except for a hoof-shaped hole. "Oh, Styx!" he mumbled.
> Rick Riordan, *The Lightning Thief*

### Tips and techniques
Rick Riordan recommends that writers use "a single deft stroke" to create characters. He says that a long "list of physical traits is realistic, but it is neither memorable nor compelling."

## CHOOSE A POINT OF VIEW

**W**ho will tell the story of your myth—its hero or another of its characters? How much do you want readers to know about the characters and what they thought and felt? Before you write your myth, you must choose a point of view or points of view for it.

### Omniscient viewpoint

Many myths are traditionally told from the all-seeing and all-knowing—the omniscient—point of view. The story-teller or narrator describes what all the characters think and feel and also shares knowledge of events beyond the characters' knowledge. The omniscient viewpoint is used in this myth told by the Apache people of the American Southwest:

*Long ago, the world was filled with evil giants and monsters who preyed on the Apache people. At that time, White-Painted Woman married the Sun. She gave birth to a boy— Child of Water—who slew the enemies of the people. White-Painted Woman watched as her son made the world safe for the Apache.*

Joseph Bruchac and Gayle Ross, "The Beauty Way—The Ceremony of White-Painted Woman," in *The Girl Who Married the Moon: Tales from Native North America*

## First-person viewpoint

The first-person viewpoint, using "I" or "we," permits readers to hear someone's inner thoughts or actual speech. *The Lightning Thief* is told from the first-person viewpoint of its hero, Percy Jackson. Here he talks with his mother:

> *I told her she was smothering me, and to lay off and all that, but secretly, I was really, really glad to see her.*
> Rick Riordan, *The Lightning Thief*

Much of the excitement in this modern retelling of Greek myths comes from its first-person viewpoint. Percy does not know important secrets about his family. Readers experience Percy's emotions and thoughts during adventures that give him this information and confidence in himself, too.

### CASE STUDY

Paul Fleischman's *Dateline: Troy* uses the omniscient viewpoint in its retelling of a conflict connected to many Greek myths. Fleischman, however, uses an unusual method to add another viewpoint to his book. On every other page, he includes articles and ads from modern newspapers that echo these ancient, bloody events. Fleischman says, "The Trojan War is still being fought. Simply open a newspaper."

### CASE STUDY

Author Clemence McLaren uses many first-person viewpoints in her myth-based novels, *Inside the Walls of Troy* and *Waiting for Odysseus*. All of her narrators are human women or goddesses involved in the Trojan War. McLaren wanted readers to hear from female characters who are often only briefly mentioned or "silenced" in myths.

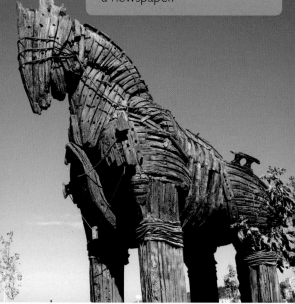

# THIRD-PERSON VIEWPOINT

**T**he third-person viewpoint follows the experiences, thoughts, and feelings of one character, who only knows what other characters think or feel by interacting with them. The myth teller refers to this narrator, who may be the hero, by the person's name and by "he" or "she."

*The Sea of Trolls* is told mainly through the third-person viewpoint of its hero, Jack:

> *Jack woke before dawn and listened to the cold February wind lash the walls of the house. He sighed. It was going to be another rotten day. He stared up at the rafters, savoring the last minutes of warmth.*
> Nancy Farmer, *The Sea of Trolls*

Sometimes, for extra drama, a storyteller includes brief bits of first-person viewpoint. Nancy Farmer does this when Jack almost freezes to death:

> *I'm not sleepy, I'm cold, thought Jack. But he found he was sleepy after all. It would feel so nice to give himself up to the sensation. He could almost see the frost giants calling to him.*
> Nancy Farmer, *The Sea of Trolls*

## Multiple third-person viewpoints

Using multiple third-person points of view is another way to add drama to your myth. In *Odysseus in the Serpent Maze*, authors Jane Yolen and Robert J. Harris shift between Odysseus' viewpoint and the view of his friend Mentor. These authors mainly use the third-person to tell each character's experience, but they also occasionally drop into the first-person to give readers each boy's thoughts.

### Now it's your turn

**View your myth carefully**

Before you decide on the point of view for your myth, experiment. Take 10 minutes to write it from the omniscient viewpoint. Now take another 10 minutes to write it from the hero's point of view.

Which version do you like more? Do you need a viewpoint beyond the knowledge of any one character to communicate all the events in the myth?

### Now it's your turn

**Seeing other points of view**

Experiment further with your choice of viewpoints. Think about your myth. Take 10 minutes to write it from the villain's point of view. Or try writing it from the viewpoint of a character on the edges of the myth. This could be a servant, relative, or shepherd already mentioned in the myth. Or you could write from the viewpoint of a child or even an animal or bird observing these events. You might gain just a few new ideas from this experiment, or you might decide to use this viewpoint for all or part of your storytelling.

## TELL YOUR STORY'S STORY

**As your story takes shape like a statue crafted by an ancient sculptor, it is a good idea to describe it in a paragraph or two. This is called a synopsis. If someone asked, "What is this myth about?" these paragraphs would be the answer. An editor often wants to see a synopsis of a story before accepting it for publication.**

### Study back cover blurbs

Studying the information on the back cover of a book—called the blurb—will help you write an effective synopsis. A good blurb contains a brief summary of a book's content. It also gives the tone of the book—whether it is serious or funny. Most important of all, the blurb makes readers want to open the book and read it cover-to-cover. That is certainly true of this blurb:

*Odysseus believed the age of heroes was over.*

*Then he and his best friend, along with a spoiled princess named Helen and her cousin Penelope, are kidnapped by pirates!*

*Their journey leads them to Crete, where Odysseus must face the secret at the heart of the Labyrinth. There was a time when the Minotaur devoured all who entered, but now an even deadlier monster roams the maze.*

*There Odysseus discovers the hardest part of being a hero: living long enough to tell the tale.*

Jane Yolen and Robert J. Harris, *Odysseus in the Serpent Maze*

### Now it's your turn

**Marketing your myth**

Write a blurb for the myth you plan to write. Summarizing it in one or two paragraphs will sharpen your ideas for this new version of an ancient story.

## Now it's your turn

**Lights! Camera! Action!**

Reread your blurb. Use it to identify the most important events in the myth. You are now ready to sketch the "scenes" for the myth's story. Under each sketched scene, jot down brief notes about what you will mention about this event.

Use this series of storyboards as a helpful outline as you write the myth. If your retelling of this story has chapters, each scene may be a separate chapter. Perhaps two or more scenes will fit together well in one chapter.

## Make a story map

One way to plan your myth is to think of it the way filmmakers prepare a movie. Before they start filming, they must know the main story episodes. They must also map out the plot (the sequence of events) in a series of sketches called storyboards. You can do this for your myth. The blurb you wrote will help you here.

## Novels versus short stories

Once you have worked out the main scenes, or episodes, in your myth, you can decide if you want to tell them briefly in a story or develop each one further as a chapter in a novel. Novels—like short stories—have heroes, villains, and conflicts. Novels have many more characters than short stories, though, and usually have subplots as well as the main plot. Just like a short story, each chapter in a novel has its own beginning, middle, and end. Sometimes chapters in a novel are told from different points of view.

## Write a chapter synopsis

Another way to plan a longer written project is to write a chapter synopsis. If your myth will be novel length, this method might help you tell it. Group major events into five to eight categories, such as the hero's childhood, earliest adventure, romance, successes, and setbacks. Use each of these categories as a chapter. Following a chapter synopsis as an outline is one helpful way to keep on track as you write.

### Tips and techniques

Write chapter titles that communicate your voice as well as content. In The Sea of Monsters, his second humor-filled book about Percy Jackson's adventures, Rick Riordan uses this technique. His chapter titles include "We Hail the Taxi of Eternal Torment" and "We Meet the Sheep of Doom."

## HOOK YOUR READERS

**N**ow that you have planned your myth, how will you catch and keep the reader's attention? You might choose a fascinating first sentence to hook readers into your work. Then reel them in with the rest of the equally exciting first paragraphs.

### Some good beginnings

The opening sentence and paragraphs could be mysterious in an entertaining way, if that voice matches the rest of your myth. That is how Laurence Yep begins his novel set in modern San Francisco:

*It isn't every day you meet a tiger. And certainly not a tiger in a suit and tie. And definitely not one who knows your first name. The tiger was the last thing Tom Lee expected as he stumbled up the steps to his grandmother's home.*
Laurence Yep, *The Tiger's Apprentice*

Your attention-grabbing sentence and opening paragraphs could be dark and mysterious, if this style better matches your myth. Paul Fleischman makes such a match with this opening:

*It began with a nightmare.*
*Hecuba, queen of Troy, was with child. The night before the birth, she awoke shrieking. "The fire!" she cried out. "It spreads!"*
*King Priam bolted up. There was no fire. Hecuba had been dreaming. Shaking, she stammered what she'd dreamt: that instead of bearing a child, she'd brought forth a tangle of flaming snakes.*
Paul Fleischman, *Dateline: Troy*

You could even grab readers' attention by speaking directly to them, as Rick Riordan does:

> *Look, I didn't want to be a half-blood.*
> *If you're reading this because you think you might be one, my advice is: close this book right now. Believe whatever lie your mom or dad told you about your birth, and try to lead a normal life.*
> *Being a half-blood is dangerous. It's scary. Most of the time, it gets you killed in painful, nasty ways.*
> Rick Riordan, *The Lightning Thief*

## CASE STUDY

Laurence Yep is an American author who writes award-winning books that reflect his Chinese roots. Chinese mythology is an important part of Yep's series of novels featuring seventh-grader Tom Lee: *The Tiger's Apprentice*, *Tiger's Blood*, and *Tiger Magic*.

### Tips and techniques

Consider listing a cast of characters at the beginning of your myth. This will help readers recognize the names of people, gods, and creatures from other traditions. Nancy Farmer provides such a list in **The Sea of Trolls**.

### Tips and techniques

Does your myth have its origin in historical events? If so, consider including this information in a preface or opening author's note. Paul Fleischman begins Dateline: Troy with a preface explaining what archaeologists today know about the ancient city of Troy.

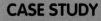

# BUILD THE SUSPENSE

**A**fter your exciting opening, do not let the excitement die. Keep and build suspense for your readers by crafting the myth in ways that emphasize the dramatic events to come.

## Thrills and chills

One way to keep readers on the edge of their seats is to place characters in a race against time. In *The Lightning Thief*, Percy and his friends must travel across the country and solve a dangerous mystery by a certain date. Every chapter mentions the decreasing number of days they have left.

You can also add suspense by hinting about unusual, unexpected, or unpleasant events that will occur in the future. This writing technique—called foreshadowing—will have readers eagerly turning pages to find out what happens next. Early in *The Lightning Thief*, a bully Percy dislikes suddenly finds herself sitting in a nearby park fountain! The seemingly magical way the water "grabbed" her in response to Percy's feelings hints at the strange events to come.

## Keeping interest high

Often, successful novelists keep up suspense by ending chapters with a cliff-hanger, like this one:

> *"Perhaps," Penelope said slowly, "it's a plague ship."*
> *"Then it'd mean possible death to board her," said Mentor.*
> *"It means* certain *death if we stay here," Odysseus said, pointing to the puddle of water spreading around his ankles.*
> Jane Yolen and Robert J. Harris, *Odysseus in the Serpent Maze*

This ending propels readers toward the next chapter to discover just what happens after this hard choice.

In these adventures of young Odysseus, the authors bring chills to knowledgeable readers in another way. Because we know the myths about adult Odysseus' dangerous travels, we shiver when the brave boy promises himself to one day "make a voyage such as no man has ever made before." Readers know that this promise will come true in ways the boy does not imagine. This technique of having characters know less than the reader—called dramatic irony—is another way to keep reader interest high.

## Character conflict

Conflict and struggle—whether internal or external—are central to the human story at the heart of your myth. In real life, however, people often experience more than one conflict at a time. The myth you are writing may have one or more subplots as well as a main plot. For example, in *The Lightning Thief,* Percy and his friend Annabeth sometimes argue because they are loyal to different Greek gods— Poseidon and Athena—who have a longstanding quarrel. In *Starfall: Phaeton and the Chariot of the Sun,* Phaeton, a teenager, becomes jealous when his sweetheart pays attention to another boy. One reason Phaeton wishes to perform daring deeds is to outshine his rival.

### Now it's your turn

**The plot thickens**

Examine each of the storyboards or chapters you are using to organize your myth. For each one, make notes to indicate any conflicts your hero or narrator experiences during that event or time. Maintain suspense by including these conflicts as you write the myth.

# END WITH A BANG

**S**tories build up suspense until they reach a climax. After that, the characters' main problems are solved. In myths, some of these solutions are extraordinary ones that the characters may not have considered or wanted. If characters do go back to their old lives, they have learned something, conquered an enemy, or overcome a weakness.

## The climax

A myth's climax is often very dramatic. Battles between gods, fights-to-the-death with terrifying monsters, and magical transformations often top off the suspense.

## Conclude your adventure

Almost everyone likes a happy ending, but believable stories—especially myths—usually do not have completely happy endings. Some problems remain in the characters' lives. In *Starfall: Phaeton and the Chariot of the Sun*, the foolishly daring Phaeton survives his ride, but he is no longer human. He has been changed by the gods into the wind. Although Phaeton is now immortal, he has lost his chance to live and love as a human.

In *The Sea of Trolls*, Jack and the Viking girl Thorgil defeat monsters and the Troll Queen. Jack and his sister return home, but they have to leave Thorgil behind, to her own life in a faraway land.

## Suggest new beginnings

A good ending often suggests that the characters, having conquered an enemy or gained new knowledge, are ready for new adventures. Having slain monsters and even survived a trip to the Underworld, Percy Jackson faces a hard choice about where to spend the next school year:

### Tips and techniques
*A good ending often links back to the beginning. This reminds readers of how much has changed during the myth.*

*I made my decision.*
*I wondered, if Poseidon were watching, would he approve of my choice?*
*"I'll be back next summer," I promised him. "I'll survive until then.*
*After all, I am your son." I asked Argus to take me down to cabin three,*
*so I could pack my bags for home.*
Rick Riordan, *The Lightning Thief*

Young Odysseus' successful adventures end with a nighttime visit from the goddess Athena. When she tells him about some of the dangers he may face as an adult, Odysseus excitedly accepts these challenges:

*Odysseus had never felt so awake in his life. He tapped the golden key*
*against his palm, grinning.*
Jane Yolen and Robert J. Harris, *Odysseus in the Serpent Maze*

## Bad endings

Create a myth of heroic propor-tions by avoiding a bad ending. Bad endings are ones that:
- fizzle out or end abruptly because you've run out of ideas,
- fail to show how the characters have changed in some way,
- are too good to be true, or
- are too grim and depressing and leave readers with no hope.

### Now it's your turn

**Choose your own ending**
Reread one of your favorite myths and think about its ending. Could it have ended in other ways? Write one of these new endings. Put it aside. Now go back and read both versions of the myth. Which one do you prefer—and why?

## MAKE YOUR WORDS WORK

**T**he right words will work wonders in your myth.
They will transport readers to faraway places and
times. Well-chosen words will also make astonishing
events, creatures, and beings seem as real as next-
door neighbors.

### A sense of life

Use as many of the five senses as possible to make descriptions come
alive. Touch as well as sight help readers experience Pan's description
of how autumn inspires his music:

*I play the shortening of late-summer days,*
*how the south wind, Notus, leaves the*
*white trumpet flowers swinging, how*
*the foxes' fur thickens. I move on,*
*day by day, week by week. I play*
*the hardwood trees, shocked at*
*the first frost, changing the color*
*of their leaves to seductive hues*
*of yellow and red, and the north*
*wind, Boreas, blowing*
*off those leaves once*
*they've shriveled to brown,*
*and the hares lining their*
*burrows with the fallen leaves.*
Donna Jo Napoli, *The Great God Pan*

### *Tips and techniques*

*A metaphor describes something by calling it some-*
*thing else—for instance, a fierce man is a "tiger."*
*A simile describes something by comparing it to*
*something with the word "like" or "as." For example,*
*a dewdrop sparkles like a diamond.*

| GETTING STARTED | SETTING THE SCENE | CHARACTERS | VIEWPOINT |

## Use vivid imagery

Bring scenes to life by creating vivid word pictures with metaphors and similes. Donna Jo Napoli uses a metaphor when Pan describes how he used bees to attack some thieves:

*Perfect. The hive swarms. Bees in the outlaws' hair and noses and mouths. Clouds of bees chase the men to their horses, horses that bolted at the first buzz.*
Donna Jo Napoli, *The Great God Pan*

This does not mean that the bees really turned into clouds but that they flew close enough together to look like clouds. This word picture communicates how dense the bee swarms were.

Mary Pope Osborne uses a simile to describe the beautiful Norse goddess Sif in a tale about "How Thor Got His Hammer":

*Made of gold, Sif's hair gleamed like summer wheat blowing in the wind. One night while Sif slept, the mischief-maker, Loki, crept into her chamber and cut off all her hair.*
Mary Pope Osborne,
*Favorite Norse Myths*

This word picture comparing Sif's hair to wheat lets readers imagine its shine and movement more vividly.

### Tips and techniques

Find and use descriptions that are common for myths in a particular tradition. The Greek storyteller Homer called the goddess of wisdom "owl-eyed Athena," saw "rosy-fingered dawn" each morning, and said sailors traveled on a "wine-dark sea."

# WRITE TO EXCITE

**W**hen you write action scenes, excite your readers with your word choice. Replace everyday action words with bold, unusual ones. Have characters race instead of run, and leap instead of jump.

Kate McMullan uses vivid action words along with a simile when Hades describes being trapped inside and then escaping from his father's stomach:

*We fought to keep our heads up as the smelly fluid sloshed over us. The whole place shook with Dad's moans and groans. Then the walls of his stomach started clenching like a giant fist. With every clench, a wave of the sour juice flew up Dad's throat. I don't know what happened next because the whirlpool sucked me down. It spun me around. Then suddenly, SPURT! I was catapulted up, up, up, up Dad's slimy gullet and—BLECCHH!—spat out into the world.* Kate McMullan, *Have a Hot Time, Hades!*

## Now it's your turn

### Soar into the sky

By yourself or with a friend, make a list of 10 everyday action words such as walk or fly. Then have fun brainstorming at least four unusual substitutes for each word. Perhaps someone would plunge instead of fall. Use a dictionary or thesaurus for extra help. Make every word count. Like an ancient storyteller, you are using words to touch people's hearts and minds.

*Now it's your turn*

**Color your sensational words**

By yourself or with a friend, brainstorm some similes for colors and textures. Make a list of 10 colors and textures. For each word, write down five similes. For instance, "As blue (or gray or green) as a … " or try "As smooth (or sharp or rough) as the … " How could you use these images or ones like them in your myth? Use a dictionary or thesaurus for extra help.

# CHAPTER 7: SCINTILLATING SPEECH

## USE DRAMATIC DIALOGUE

**D**ialogue lets readers "hear" characters as they speak. It helps readers understand different personalities and the relationships between people. Dialogue also gives readers' eyes a rest as it breaks up the page of narrative (storytelling). Done well, dialogue is a powerful storytelling tool—one that adds color, mood, and suspense even as it moves the plot forward.

### Let your characters speak for themselves

Early in *The Sea of Trolls*, Jack hears his 5-year-old sister Lucy and their parents:

> *"It's so **cold**," complained Lucy from the loft. "Can't I have breakfast in bed?"*
> *"A princess isn't afraid of a little thing like cold," said Father.*
> *"Princesses live in castles," Lucy pointed out.*
> *"Ah, but that isn't true of **lost** princesses."*
> *"Don't encourage her," said Mother.*
> *"Am I really lost, Father?" said Lucy. Jack knew she loved this story.*
> *"Not for long. You were found by us," Father said fondly.*
> *"I was lying under a rose tree with a gold coin in my hand." ...*
> *"Someday the knights will knock at our door," said Lucy. "They'll bow to me and say, 'Come and be our queen.'"*
> Nancy Farmer, *The Sea of Trolls*

Lucy's belief in this fairy tale leads to disaster when Vikings raid her family's small farming community. Her belief also figures later in the novel's plot. This dialogue shows why Lucy believes she is a princess and helps readers understand Lucy and her family.

## Now it's your turn

### Listen in

Tune in to the way people talk. Turn on the radio or TV for 10 minutes, and copy down bits of conversation. Or jot down what you overhear on a train or bus or in an elevator or store. You will begin to notice how people often have favorite expressions and different rhythms to their speech. Sometimes someone may not wait to talk until the other person is finished. How can you use these different speech patterns in the dialogue you write?

## Follow convention

Dialogue is usually written down according to certain rules. Each new speaker begins a new paragraph. You already know that what a person actually said is enclosed in quotation marks, followed or preceded by a tag such as "he said" or "she said." Sometimes, to give the sense of a real conversation, writers place these tags in the middle of a sentence. This placement adds another rhythm to the conversation, making it more lifelike.

### Tips and techniques

Use say, said, or wrote to introduce quotations. You can sometimes substitute words such as complained, whispered, or shouted for variety or when they suit the situation.

# ADDING COLOR AND MOOD

**C**hristopher Tebbetts uses dialogue to add color to the adventures of Zack Gilman, a modern high school freshman who meets the Norse gods and their creatures:

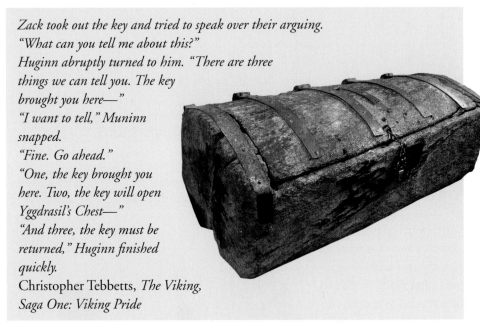

*Zack took out the key and tried to speak over their arguing.*
*"What can you tell me about this?"*
*Huginn abruptly turned to him. "There are three things we can tell you. The key brought you here—"*
*"I want to tell," Muninn snapped.*
*"Fine. Go ahead."*
*"One, the key brought you here. Two, the key will open Yggdrasil's Chest—"*
*"And three, the key must be returned," Huginn finished quickly.*
Christopher Tebbetts, *The Viking, Saga One: Viking Pride*

This overlapping dialogue shows how competitive these fantastic creatures—giant, information-gathering ravens—are. Dialogue also creates a comic mood when Zack tries to have a conversation in a noisy place:

*"Good morning!" Jok roared over the pounding hammers.*
*"Listen," Zack shouted. "I was wondering—"*
*"Thundering, yes!" Jok yelled back. "Quite a noise!"*
*"No," said Zack. "I was **wondering**. Can we row back to where you found me?"*
*"Pounding?"*
*"No! Where you found me!"*
*Jok shook his head and Zack sat down to wait.*
Christopher Tebbetts, *The Viking, Saga One: Viking Pride*

Jok's misunderstandings here create humor in this scene.

### Now it's your turn

**As she was saying …**

Reread your myth. Are there parts of the narrative that could be better told in dialogue? Rewrite a scene using or adding dialogue. If they are appropriate, use overlapping statements or humor. Now set both versions of the myth aside. Go back later and see which version you like more.

# USE DIFFERENT VOICES

**W**riting dialogue is a challenge even for experienced, skilled writers. Remember that characters should not sound like you. Rick Riordan also advises writers that "No two characters should sound the same." How characters speak often reveals a great deal about their background.

## Social class

Odysseus speaks like an uneducated farmer to keep his royal background a secret:

> *"We was chasing a sow who run off, great lord," answered Odysseus, being careful not to look right into the captain's eyes. "My mate and me."*
> Jane Yolen and Robert J. Harris, *Odysseus in the Serpent Maze*

## Foreign accent

The speech of Heide, a wise woman from Finnmark, shows that she comes from a land faraway from the Viking village where captive Jack meets her:

> *"I like thiss boy," she announced in a heavily accented voice.*
> *"Now, Heide, I'm not giving him to you," said Olaf.*
> *"You haff not the giffing uff this boy," Heide said.*
> *"And you have not the getting, woman. See, I brought you a pot of herbs and medicines, as you asked."*
> Nancy Farmer, *The Sea of Trolls*

### Tips and techniques
If your character has an accent, do not try to reproduce it exactly. Suggest it by the way the speech is phrased, by spelling an everyday word differently, or by including a foreign word in a greeting or excited remark.

## Now it's your turn

**Compress your dialogue**

Try removing tags such as "he said" or "she shouted" from your dialogue. Does the pace of the conversation seem more natural? Does this pace better suit the mood and purpose of the scene? Can you still identify who is speaking? Some scenes work better with compressed dialogue that has no tags. If you cannot tell who is speaking without tags, you may want to work more to develop each character's voice.

## Mythological origin

Grover's speech contains traces of the secret identity Percy has just discovered:

> "It doesn't matter? From the waist down, my best friend is a donkey—"
> Grover let out a sharp, throaty
> **"Blaa-ha-ha!"**
> I'd heard him make that sound before, but I'd always assumed it was a nervous laugh. Now I realized it was more of an irritated bleat.
> "Goat!" he cried.
> "What?"
> "I'm a **goat** from the waist down."
> "You just said it didn't matter."
> **"Blaa-ha-ha!** There are satyrs who would trample you underhoof for such an insult!"
> Rick Riordan, *The Lightning Thief*

### Tips and techniques

Watch out! Your slang may not fit well into a myth set long ago or faraway. "Cool" expressions become outdated quickly, too.

## BEAT WRITER'S BLOCK

**E**ven famous writers sometimes get stuck for words or ideas. This is called writer's block. If you have been following the writer's golden rule (writing regularly and often), you already have some ways to battle writer's block. Here are some of its causes and other weapons to use.

### Your inner critic

Do not listen to that inner voice that might whisper negative ideas about your writing. All writers try out and then throw away some of their efforts. Paul Fleischman says he spends "as much time on thinking out the story as on the actual writing." He believes he learned from his "many mistakes and false starts" and says he is "still learning."

### No ideas

Have you run out of ideas? Joseph Bruchac tells young writers to "forget about writer's block. Just sit down and start writing, and sooner or later you'll find something worth saying."

Bruce Coville—whose many novels include *Thor's Wedding Day*, his retelling of a Norse myth—has another recommendation. Coville

> **Tips and techniques**
> Get inspiration and new ideas by examining different writers' versions of the same myth or mythical character.

encourages writers to "write down ideas when they come to you. The human brain is cranky. If you want an idea your mind will probably refuse to give it to you. But if you are doing something else, sometimes ideas just come floating by. The trick is to save ideas when they come to you."

Be inspired by the efforts of other myth writers. Seeing the different ways that authors have told the same myth may be particularly useful. For instance, both Bruce Coville and Mary Pope Osborne have written about the Norse god Thor.

# LEARN THE TRICKS OF THE TRADE

## A writers' group

Writing may seem lonely. Some writers take heart by sharing their works-in-progress with other writers. They meet regularly in person or over the Internet with "writing buddies." These critique groups help fight writer's block by sharing ideas, experiences, and even goals. Bruce Coville meets monthly with a critique group, whose members also take some time to gossip and eat. Rick Riordan shared his works-in-progress with his sons and with the middle school students he used to teach.

## A change of pace

Defeat writer's block by changing your writing habits. If you normally brainstorm sitting still, try walking instead. If you usually like quiet while you write, add music to your myth-writing zone. If you write at the computer, try pen and paper. Vary your writing habits for each stage of the process. Jane Yolen does a lot of research and thinking in the quiet attic of her Massachusetts home, where she often has visitors. But she writes her myth-centered books at her second home in Scotland. Her co-writer Robert J. Harris is a neighbor there.

### Now it's your turn

**Slay the writer's block monster**

Start a writer's group with other writers, or partner up with a writing buddy. Set a regular meeting time and place, and talk about how much new work you will bring to meetings. Slay that monster together.

## NOW WHAT?

**C**ongratulations! Completing your own myth is a great achievement. You have learned a lot about writing and probably about yourself, too. You are now ready to take the next step in creating wonderful new stories.

### Another myth?

While researching this myth, you might have discovered another one that fascinates you. Perhaps a mythological character or fantastic creature from a different tradition caught your attention. Your next writing project might be another myth based on these discoveries.

### How about a prequel or sequel?

Is there more to tell about the characters in your myth? Perhaps, like Jane Yolen and Robert J. Harris, you are interested in writing about the early life of heroic characters. Your next project could be such a prequel. Perhaps there are many more adventures ahead of an original character you created and put into a mythic setting. Rick Riordan has already written two books about Percy Jackson and plans to write three more sequels.

### Write a related myth or other work

Perhaps one of the settings or historical events in your myth caught your imagination. You might want to spin a new myth using one of these settings or events. Or you might decide to do further research and write a historical fiction story focusing on people and events in that faraway time and place. You might want to write a biography—the real-life story—of someone who lived then.

*Now it's your turn*

**Imagine that!**

Brainstorm your next story with pen and paper. Think of a myth you enjoyed reading. List five things that might have happened to the hero or creatures there before or after the events described in the myth. Do not worry about punctuation or grammar as you jot down ideas. Repeat this process with another myth. When you are done, you may have found the characters and plot for your next writing project.

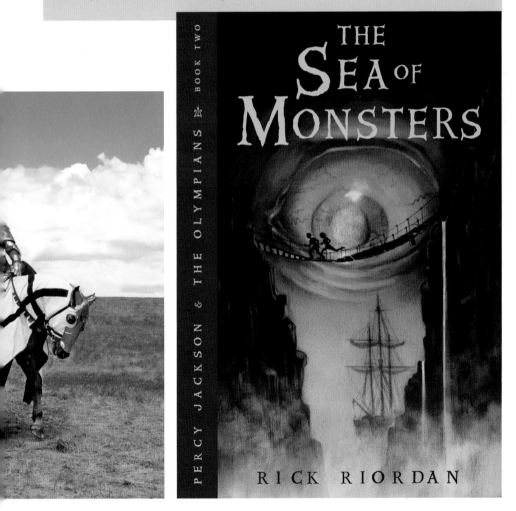

PERCY JACKSON & THE OLYMPIANS 🔱 BOOK TWO

THE SEA OF MONSTERS

RICK RIORDAN

# LEARN FROM THE AUTHORS

**Y**ou can learn a great deal from the advice of successful writers. Almost all will tell you that hard work and occasional failure are part of the writing lifestyle. Yet even though few writers earn enough from their books to make a living, they value their ability to create and communicate through written words.

## Jane Yolen

After college, Jane Yolen (left) worked in publishing as an editor. She has since written and published more than 200 books. The idea for the Young Heroes series of books came from her editor, but Yolen and Robert J. Harris made the decision to "have both boy and girl heroes" in these prequels to mythical adventures.

Yolen says she has "three pieces of advice for young writers. One: read, read, read! You must read every day, and try to read a wide range of books. Two: write, write, write! Keep a journal, write letters, anything to keep the 'writing muscles' in shape. Three: Don't let anyone stop you from writing. Be persistent no matter what 'naysayers' or critical editors have to say about your writing."

## Rick Riordan

Rick Riordan (right) began writing seriously when he was in eighth grade, after a teacher encouraged him to submit work for publication. He urges young writers to "ask for help. Find a teacher you respect. Correspond with authors. You will find that a polite e-mail will almost always get a response."

Besides advising young writers to read and write a lot, Riordan tells them not to get discouraged. He reminds them, "Rejection is a part of writing, and it hurts. The trick is to keep at it. Wallpaper your room with rejection notes, if you want, but don't give up."

## Joseph Bruchac

Joseph Bruchac did not let criticism discourage him. A college writing teacher told him to give up writing because he would never write a good poem. "From that point on," Bruchac says, "I literally ate, slept, and dreamed poetry." Today he is the author of more than 70 published books.

# PREPARE YOUR WORK

**L**et your myth rest in your desk drawer or on a shelf for several weeks. Then, when you read it through, you will have fresh eyes to spot any flaws.

## Think of a title

Great titles capture the reader's interest. They not only indicate the subject of the book but also make the reader want to learn more about it. *The Lightning Thief* and *The Sea of Monsters* are more compelling titles than *The Adventures of Percy Jackson*. Sometimes titles also indicate the author's voice. Kate McMullan's title, *Have a Hot Time, Hades!*, reflects the joking and casual way she retells this Greek myth. Her entertaining sequels to this work also have fun-filled titles, such as *Keep a Lid on It, Pandora!* and *Phone Home, Persephone!*

## Edit your work

Reading your work aloud is one way to make the writing crisper. Now is the time to check spelling and punctuation. When the myth is as good as it can be, write it out again or type it up on the computer. This is your manuscript.

## Be professional

If you have a computer, you can type up your manuscript to give it a professional presentation. Manuscripts should always be printed on one side of white paper, with wide margins and double spacing. Pages should be numbered, and new chapters should start on a new page. You should also include your title as a header on the top of each page. At the front, you should have a title page with your name, address, telephone number, and e-mail address on it. Repeat this information on the last page.

## Make your own book

If your school has its own computer lab, why not use it to publish your myth? A computer will let you choose your own font (print style) or justify the text (making margins even like a professionally printed page). When you have typed and saved the myth to a file, you can edit it quickly with the spelling and grammar checker, or move sections around using the cut-and-paste tool, which saves a lot of rewriting. A graphics program will let you design and print a cover for the book, too.

Having the myth on a computer file also means you can print a copy whenever you need one or revise the whole myth if you want to.

### Tips and techniques
*Always make a copy of your myth before you give it to others to read. Otherwise, if they lose it, you may have lost all your valuable work.*

# REACH YOUR AUDIENCE

The next step is to find an audience for your myth. Family members or classmates may be receptive. Read it to your younger brother or sister. Members of a community group representing the tradition your myth is from might like to read your work. Or you may want to share your work through a Web site, a literary magazine, or a publishing house.

## Some places to publish your myth

There are several magazines and writing Web sites that accept myths from young authors. Some give writing advice and run regular competitions. Each site has its own rules about submitting work, so remember to read these carefully. Here are two more ideas:

- Send the myth to your school newspaper.
- Watch your local newspaper or magazines for writing competitions you could enter.

## Finding a publisher

Study the market to find out which publishers publish myths. Addresses of publishers and information about whether they accept submissions can be found in writers' handbooks in the library. Keep in mind that manuscripts that haven't been asked for or paid for by a publisher—called unsolicited manuscripts—are rarely published. Secure any submission with a staple or paper clip and always enclose a short letter (explaining what you have sent) and a stamped, self-addressed envelope for the myth's return.

### Tips and techniques
*Don't lose heart if an editor rejects your myth. See this as a chance to make your work better and try again. Remember, having your work published is wonderful, but it is not the only thing. Being able to write a myth is an accomplishment that will delight the people you love.*

## Some final words

Writing a myth brings you closer to the creative energy shown by people for thousands of years. It shows you how—despite their differences—people around the world are fascinated by the same great mysteries in life. It also helps you think about and understand a bit more about why people behave as they do. With this success and knowledge, you are ready to tackle the next wonderful challenge in your life!

## Read! Write!

And keep that sense of wonder alive.

## Glossary

**chapter synopsis**—an outline that describes briefly what happens in each chapter

**cliff-hanger**—ending a chapter or scene of a story at a nail-biting moment

**dramatic irony**—when the reader knows something the characters don't

**edit**—to remove all unnecessary words from your story, correcting errors, and rewriting the text until the story is the best it can be

**editor**—the person at a publishing house who finds new books to publish and advises authors on how to improve their stories by telling them what needs to be added or cut

**first-person viewpoint**—a viewpoint that allows a single character to tell the story as if he or she had written it; readers feel as if that character is talking directly to them

**foreshadowing**—dropping hints of coming events or dangers that are essential to the outcome of the story

**genres**—categories of writing characterized by a particular style, form, or content

**manuscript**—book or article typed or written by hand

**metaphor**—a figure of speech that paints a word picture; calling a man "a mouse" is a metaphor from which we learn in one word that the man is timid or weak, not that he is actually a mouse

**motives**—the reasons why a character does something

**narrative**—the telling of a story

**omniscient viewpoint**—an all-seeing narrator who can describe all the characters and tell readers how they are acting and feeling

**plot**—the sequence of events that drives a story forward; the problems that the hero must resolve

**point of view**—the eyes through which a story is told

**prequel**—events that occur to characters before they appear in an existing story

**publisher**—a person or company who pays for an author's manuscript to be printed as a book and who distributes and sells that book

**sequel**—a story that carries an existing one forward

**simile**—saying something is like something else; a word picture, such as "clouds like frayed lace"

**synopsis**—short summary that describes what a story is about and introduces the main characters

**third-person viewpoint**—a viewpoint that describes the events of the story through a single character's eyes

**unsolicited manuscripts**—manuscripts that are sent to publishers without being requested; these submissions usually end up in the "slush pile," where they may wait a long time to be read

**writer's block**—when writers think they can no longer write or have used up all their ideas

## Further information

Visit your local libraries and make friends with the librarians. They can direct you to useful sources of information, including magazines that publish young people's myths. You can learn your craft and read great stories at the same time.

Librarians will also know if any published authors are scheduled to speak in your area. Many authors visit schools and offer writing workshops. Ask your teacher to invite a favorite author to speak at your school.

### On the Web

For more information on this topic, use FactHound.

1. Go to www.facthound.com
2. Type in this book ID: 0756533724
3. Click on the *Fetch It* button.

FactHound will find the best Web sites for you.

### Read all the Write Your Own books

*Write Your Own Adventure Story*
*Write Your Own Biography*
*Write Your Own Fairy Tale*
*Write Your Own Fantasy Story*
*Write Your Own Historical Fiction Story*
*Write Your Own Mystery Story*
*Write Your Own Myth*
*Write Your Own Realistic Fiction Story*
*Write Your Own Science Fiction Story*
*Write Your Own Tall Tale*

### Read more myths

Barth, Edna. *Cupid and Psyche: A Love Story.* New York: Seabury Press, 1976.

Bruchac, Joseph. *Between Earth & Sky: Legends of Native American Sacred Places.* San Diego: Harcourt Brace Jovanovich, 1996.

Coville, Bruce. *Thor's Wedding Day, By Thialfi, the Goat Boy.* Orlando: Harcourt, 2005.

D'Aulaire, Ingri. *Ingri and Edgar Parin D'Aulaire's Book of Greek Myths.* Garden City, N.Y.: Doubleday, 1962.

Gates, Doris. *The Golden God: Apollo.* New York: Penguin Books, 1983.

Hepplewhite, Peter. *The Adventures of Perseus.* Minneapolis: Compass Point Books, 2005.

Keenan, Sheila. *Gods, Goddesses, and Monsters: A Book of World Mythology.* New York: Scholastic, 2003.

Low, Alice. *The Macmillan Book of Greek Gods and Heroes.* New York: Aladdin Books, 1994.

Malam, John. *Jason and the Argonauts.* Minneapolis: Compass Point Books, 2005.

Mayo, Gretchen Will. *Star Tales: North American Indian Stories About the Stars.* New York: Walker, 1987.

McDermott, Gerald. *Daughter of Earth: A Roman Myth.* New York: Delacorte, 1984.

McLaren, Clemence. *Inside the Walls of Troy: A Novel of the Women Who Lived the Trojan War.* New York: Simon Pulse, 2004.

McLaren, Clemence. *Waiting for Odysseus.* New York: Atheneum, 2000.

Philip, Neil. *Illustrated Book of Myths.* New York: DK Children, 1995.

Reid, Sue. *The Voyages of Odysseus.* Minneapolis: Compass Point Books, 2005.

Riordan, Rick. *The Sea of Monsters.* New York: Hyperion Books, 2006.

Wilkinson, Philip. *Illustrated Dictionary of Mythology: Heroes, Heroines, Gods and Goddesses from Around the World.* New York: DK Publishing, 1998.

Yolen, Jane, and Robert J. Harris. *Atalanta and the Arcadian Beast.* New York: HarperCollins, 2003.

## Books cited

Bruchac, Joseph, and Gayle Ross. *The Girl Who Married the Moon: Tales from Native North America*. Mahwah, N.J.: Troll Associates, 1994.

Bruchac, Joseph, and Gayle Ross. *The Story of the Milky Way: A Cherokee Tale*. New York: Dial Books, 1995.

Cadmun, Michael. *Starfall: Phaeton and the Chariot of the Sun*. New York: Orchard Scholastic, 2004.

Farmer, Nancy. *The Sea of Trolls*. New York: Atheneum Books for Young Readers, 2004.

Fleischman, Paul. *Dateline: Troy*. Rev. ed. Cambridge, Mass.: Candlewick Press, 2006.

Hamilton, Virginia. *In the Beginning: Creation Stories from Around the World*. San Diego: Harcourt Brace Jovanovich, 1988.

McMullan, Kate. *Have a Hot Time, Hades!* New York: Hyperion, 2002.

Napoli, Donna Jo. *The Great God Pan*. New York: Random House, 2003.

Osborne, Mary Pope. *Favorite Norse Myths*. New York: Scholastic, 1996.

Riordan, Rick. *The Lightning Thief*. New York: Hyperion Books, 2005.

Tebbetts, Christopher. *The Viking: Saga One, Viking Pride*. New York: Puffin Penguin, 2003.

Yep, Laurence. *The Tiger's Apprentice: Book One*. New York: HarperCollins, 2003.

Yolen, Jane, and Robert J. Harris. *Odysseus in the Serpent Maze*. New York: HarperCollins, 2001.

## Image credits

# Index